How to use this book ⭑

Follow the advice, in italics, given for you on each page.
Support the children as they read the text that is shaded in cream.
Praise *the children at every step!*
Detailed guidance is provided in the Read Write Inc. Phonics Handbook.

---

9 reading activities
Children:
1 *Practise reading the speed sounds.*
2 *Read the green, red and challenge words for the non-fiction text.*
3 *Listen as you read the introduction.*
4 *Discuss the vocabulary check with you.*
5 *Read the non-fiction text.*
6 *Re-read the non-fiction text and discuss the 'questions to talk about'.*
7 *Re-read the non-fiction text with fluency and expression.*
8 *Answer the questions to 'read and answer'.*
9 *Practise reading the speed words.*

Speed sounds

Consonants Say the pure sounds (do not add 'uh').

f ff ph	l ll le	m mm mb	n nn kn	r rr wr	s ss se c ce	v (ve)	z zz se s	sh	th	ng nk

b bb	c k ck	d dd	g gg	h	j g ge	p pp	qu	t tt	w (wh)	x	y	ch tch

Vowels Say the vowel sound and then the word, eg 'a', 'at'.

at	hen head	in	on	up	day make	see tea happy he	high smile lie find	blow home no

zoo brute blue	look	car	for door snore yawn	fair care	whirl nurse letter	shout cow	boy spoil

4 *Each box contains one sound but sometimes more than one grapheme. Focus graphemes are **circled**.*

Green words

Read in Fred Talk (pure sounds).

huge	crew	stew	few	blue	safe	life	drive
ice	rice	white	flight	check	watch	air	leave
have	listen	pilot	co-pilot				

Read in syllables.

stew` ards → stew ards     air` port → airport

pass` port → passport     cock` pit → cockpit

diff` er` ent → different   diff` i` cult → difficult

ex` plore → explore     Heath` row → Heathrow

Read the root word first and then with the ending.

rule → rules   cube → cubes   tune → tunes

take → takes   place → places   cloud → clouds

amuse → amused   screen → screened

Red words

all are come here the

to you your yourself some

A flight to New York

Introduction

Have you heard of New York?
It's a big city in America.
To get there you can fly in an
aeroplane. Have you ever flown
in a plane? Have you ever been
to an airport? This book is all
about going on a journey
by plane.

Written by Gill Munton

Vocabulary check

Discuss the meaning (as used in the non-fiction text) after the children have read the word.

	definition
air crew	*people who see to your needs on an aircraft*
check in	*hand in your bags*
cockpit	*the part of the aircraft where the pilot sits*
co-pilot	*the assistant pilot*
life jackets	*blow-up jackets for a landing on water*
passport	*small book with your name and photograph inside that shows which country you come from*
screened	*checked to make sure that you are not carrying anything dangerous*
X-ray	*a photograph which shows the inside of something*

Punctuation to note:

New York	*Capital letters for names*
co-pilot X-ray	*Hyphen to link two words together*

This is Heathrow Airport.

You can take flights to 180 different places from here.

You can drive to the airport and leave your car in the huge car park.

First, you must check in your bags.

Then you must show your passport.

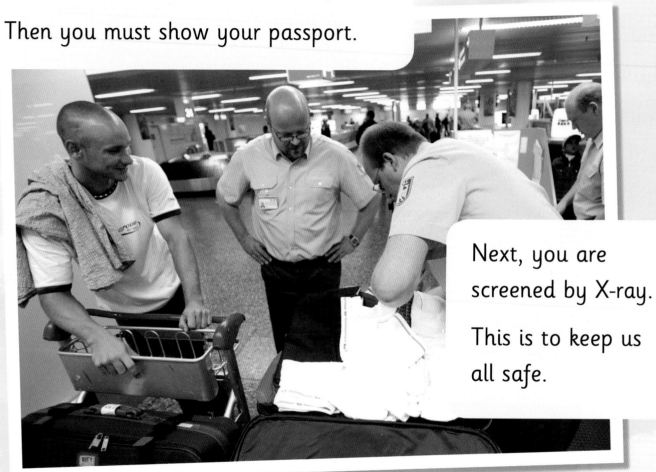

Next, you are screened by X-ray.

This is to keep us all safe.

The aircraft is huge. You have to go up some steps.

The air crew show you the life jackets and tell you the rules for a difficult landing.

You put on your seat belt and then the aircraft takes off.

Stewards come round with food and drinks on a trolley.

You can have tea or coffee, or a cool drink with ice cubes in it.

Then you have a hot meal such as stew with rice.

This is the cockpit.
The pilot and the co-pilot sit here.

On the flight, you can read to keep yourself amused.

You can listen to a few tunes, or watch a film.

Or you can just look out of the window.

The sky looks bright blue and the clouds are white and fluffy.

At the end of the flight, the aircraft lands on the runway.

This aircraft is landing in New York in America.

You go down the steps and collect your bags.

Now you can go and explore New York.

Questions to talk about

Re-read the page. Read the question to the children. Tell them whether it is a FIND IT question or PROVE IT question.

FIND IT	PROVE IT
✓ *Turn to the page*	✓ *Turn to the page*
✓ *Read the question*	✓ *Read the question*
✓ *Find the answer*	✓ *Find your evidence*
	✓ *Explain why*

Page 9:	PROVE IT	*Why do lots of people go to Heathrow Airport?*
Page 12	PROVE IT	*What do you wear while the aircraft takes off?*
Page 12:	FIND IT	*What do the stewards use to bring you drinks and meals?*
Page 14:	FIND IT	*How can you keep amused during the flight?*
Page 14:	FIND IT	*What might you see from an aircraft window?*
Page 16:	PROVE IT	*What must you remember to do before you leave the airport?*

Questions to read and answer

(Children complete without your help.)

1 What do you do first at the airport?

2 What rules do the air crew tell you about?

3 Where does the co-pilot sit?

4 What sort of things can you do on the flight?

5 Where is New York?